Blood Moon

poems

Blood Moon

poems

ANDREW JARVIS

HOMEBOUND PUBLICATIONS
Ensuring the Mainstream isn't the Only Stream

Homebound Publications
Ensuring the mainstream isn't the only stream
WWW.HOMEBOUNDPUBLICATIONS.COM

Published in 2018 • Homebound Publications
Front Cover Image © Celso
Cover and Interior Designed by Leslie M. Browning
ISBN • 978-1-947003-91-0
First Edition Trade Paperback

10 9 8 7 6 5 4 3 2 1

Homebound Publications is committed to ecological stewardship. We greatly value the
natural environment and invest in environmental conservation. Our books are printed
on paper with chain of custody certification from the Forest Stewardship Council,
Sustainable Forestry Initiative, and the Program for the
Endorsement of Forest Certification.

For Betty

Contents

Red Tide

Shadow

Burning

The Wake

Here is horizon, the rising
of bears after hibernation,

birds migrating from hemispheres,
wolves waking in ominous light,

while engineers arrive at dawn,
a welcoming of heavy work.

A pouring of population
for awesome city, a warming

feeling of hope for workers
who survive on cement, setting

water and powder adhesive
across forested floor, they rise.

With animals watching in awe,
wondering if sleep will winter

in the curious wakening
of human arrival, the rout

of solitary life, they seize
uncertainty, in existence.

Safari

The boy has dandelion eyes,
green pupils and golden eyelids,
to see sky scrape ground in color.

He weaves glasses of stems, rolling
into visions of zebras,
water buffalo, and giraffes

around a hot watering hole,
with huge hippopotami eyes
that watch rhinos bathing in blue.

Elephants blow water with trunks
that wave within safari day,
a great sighting of animals

through his floral binoculars
that focus on lions, silent
creatures, creeping for fresh lunch.

And they conquer him, attacking
body in anaphylactic
shock, yet he refuses to leave

these overgrown weeds by saving
himself with a syringe rifle,
living in shooting desire.

Moon Highway

Setting Snoqualmie
in land exchanged
for layered concrete,
life is paved over.

And glistening, it will
roundabout death,
sacred and significant,
burying moon birth.

Planned path, it opens
the flat to falls,
like water fighting,
losing to land matte.

Sand, silt, cemented
ancestors in sludge,
we watch fathers form
into lanes, expressed.

And driving to water,
they accelerate steam
and evaporate us,
like smoking the sun.

The Plan

Welcome
        to watching
awesome
        division
of forest
        and floor,
where trees
        stump
from new
        nothing.
Squirrels,
        the squealing
of them,
        and rats run
in good
        riddance, gone
like clouds
        in sonic boom,
grounding
        sound shake.
Open it up,
        eye new
city in
        clearing,
evergreens
        into taverns
and paper
        mills, mulch

for a surveyor's
        muse.
Concrete
        stands through
stained
        walls, reindeer
and raccoons
        watching
the building
        of night
into acrylic
        day, sealed.
And shining,
        it curves
into reflecting
        pools
and visitors
        centers
to unravel
        its making,
indigenous
        roots.

Solidarity

Populated by pines,
a city sustained
by an army of boughs,
this is a wooded wall

protected by the bark
of it, like incessant
doorways, unopened
and lacking a locksmith.

A man is constructing
a landscape of mansions,
making floorboards of wood,
planked by this temple

of tormented needles,
removed for rising
homes, a hauling away
by this worker, for want.

And then he throws, his back
turning into a beast of pain,
like absent opioids
in a forest of spikes

where innumerable
axe his axing with roots,
making tools of his tools,
standing tall, and growing.

Bridge Prints

Peaks, as if muddy gods
stole ground to support sky,
they run up to heaven
in great waving towers,
with shoes printed on them.

They have been walked over,
smashed into dirt pillars
of conifers, caking
overworked men, heavy
soles mounded, smoldering.

Pristine, polished, the bridge
shines like a museum,
a government project
to gift the working class
something to walk over.

With a pathetic plaque
carved into a stone wall,
it describes history,
a formal foundation,
and even chairmen wives.

Their hands wave at water,
a river beneath them,
with great mountains above,
where workers have printed
postcards, footed the bill.

Earthquake

It stole sunset, the beast below living,
        licking the loss of familial dreams:
nuclear, an exposé of mushroom puff.
        Staircases lean into labyrinth steps,
their rising reclaimed in concrete, wasting
        an attic of childhood memories.
Ballet shoes, baseballs, electric guitars,
        a mother's treadmill and father's old axe,
everything absorbed in grounded swallow.
        Lights flash around a blockade, enticing
onlookers, like insects blinking in night,
        tragedy brightened in land's sacrifice.
Beckoning you to lineage, their line
        is drawn into erasure; you are sucked
into it, their orb blooming in ending.

Forged

Come friends, find life in the living:
bodies framed into sun shadows.

Heat onto heavy work, we burn
beneath gold fire, our branding.

Shovels, milk yokes, a rusted rake,
they sweat us for blood money, spent.

In the burning, day sets on us,
boiling skin out to flood in.

Like iron alloyed with carbon,
we fuse into human steel.

Unbreakable in our making,
the molded light, we steep in shine.

Farrier

The horseshoes followed him
through the house, the nails
greeting him at the front,
picks peeking through the door.

The nippers were behind
in a great hall of rasps,
pull-offs, and clinch cutters,
leading to his hammers.

They hook the bedroom wall
above a framed anvil;
he likes their beaten heads,
the hammering hours.

Shoes, fitted to his size,
he has a pair of them,
to be fashionable
within horse heaven.

An angel will love him,
smitten by holy hooves,
his wardrobe of horses,
shoeing him, riding home.

Identity

Fishing is a fetish
for him, that casting man
with a bottle of worms

that slither in leeches,
latched to a beloved
vest, a red covering

of anchored trophies,
collected by catches
in this eternal net

of evanescent time,
where trout become hours
of mired enigmas

that spawn into swimming
labyrinths, where he snares
subaquatic treasures,

fish in underwater
bounty, as if sublime,
anointing an angler.

Skins

Men are skinning our cow,
citing our need for hide,

for the leather of it.
It pays, along with meat,

black and tan, even white;
they kill it for color.

The sight of it, the sheen
of boots and belts, it soothes

in jackets, caressing.
They wrap with wonderful.

While screaming, they shot it,
cut off the head for horns.

But left the beef, they leave
while we digest their tracks.

Steel Maiden

A shackled woman in steel,
she refuses to be unbound,
her blood flooding silver with red.

While sinking in farmland swallow,
she fights builders for belonging,
to prove lifelines are permanent.

She hammers the whole of herself
to pound workmen into earthworms,
as if nailing them to waste.

The broken, the healed, the hope,
her everything anchored, entrenched,
she disallows her good riddance.

In her, the tractors disembowel
her body to an embedded
seep into earth, an overbear.

Sinking, she welcomes the feel
of fighting, her death in home dive,
a stake into the heart of it.

Sensual Aria

He is running a skunk
around every girl,
as if exposing his
own private spectacle
with an unpleasant smell

and flares of black and white,
before batting a slide
with its pulverized
body, an opera
of symphonic stenches

and bacterial hair
that mush into a muse
of hyperbolic play,
an eruption of sound
into stinking music,

to be a loud tenor,
center of attention,
with a barbaric blow
in the stampeding wind
of the unpopular.

Shatter

So many
        in the mirror,
animals
        stuffed
like a disease
        of father,
with multiple
        fists.
Parrots
        rusting
from red
        to brown,
elephants
        graying
into black,
        they reflect
the fighting
        of him.
The frustration,
        the flying
milk, hammering
        of metronome
hands, he
        handed over
everything.
        Even these
beasts, his
        excuses

for crying
         in every
day, she
         always
accepted
         softness.
All fuzzy,
         even
flamingos
         appear
in his pink
         reflection,
sounding like
         the slapping
of him.
         Disobeying,
she blinds
         baboons
and shatters
         glass,
embracing
         escape,
into silver
         lining.

Sugar Shock

The orbit of the bee, so sweet,
she watches it working in waves
of pollen, in pulsating gold.

As if an elaborate gift,
she reaches for the shine of it,
tempted by its soaring treasure.

Allergic, she knows, but she craves
everything eaten before:
lollipops, jellybeans, and juice.

Without a sting, the bee descends
onto cream, caught by sultry silk,
the feel of floating, caressed.

She swallows it, without breaking
off the wings, as if an ogre
unfurled in her, shocked appetite.

It falls into obesity,
a girl's adolescent body,
beckoning sudden disaster.

It plunges into her, the walls
of a belly being beaten;
she dies of sugar, from its spike.

Weeping

Mother specializes in rain,
defines our weakening willows

as sponges that swallow cloud tears,
great urns for overcast ashes.

Dropping to deciduous leaves,
shimmering green into yellow,

water awakens the crying,
colors drowning in soggy brown.

Where earthquakes shatter the sinking,
dismantle them in lava gold,

burning from outer to inner,
coring the hot life of the earth.

To the opposite side where trees
bend back at us in their own storm,

leaving us in polarized flood,
praying for wet liquidation.

Storming

Mother
        manipulates
                cloud bursts,
                        as if a witch
is expelling
        the sun
                to storm
                        the light
of it.
        She streaks
                it for us, forked
                        into sky fire,
struck
        by our becoming
                rod, its metal
                        beckoning.
Maddening,
        like music without
                a common time,
                        it is striking
off key,
        sharp notes
                muted
                        by flats.
She teaches
        us torment,
                the tune
                        of sky

temper,
　　　　its chaotic
　　　　　　　soundings
　　　　　　　　　　orchestrated
to pitch
　　　　our night
　　　　　　　predicament:
　　　　　　　　　　awake
in nightmare
　　　　fall, turbulence
　　　　　　　of summer,
　　　　　　　　　　spells of anger,
piercing.

Mercy

Wind catcher convulsing
within shattering storm,
as if cursed by gods
of winged removal,
shear in acidic rain

pour on airborne body
of a falcon in arms.
A boy is watching it
with telescopic eyes,
focusing on feathers,

primaries in sky shock
like a birded plaster
of blackening, off-white.
He reaches, fights flying
to grant land to aloft,

as if recalling air
for bird asphyxia;
and he strangles it,
to stop its flyaway,
stunning, beaten, breathless.

From Water

Mother swallowed the street,
drank it in the drowning

of historical homes,
white pickets swept to clear.

Gardens of grown delights,
with seagulls sunk over,

they washed into her well
of life, her flooded core.

Playgrounds, churches, and schools
swelled like oceans in squall,

drooping in displacement,
with sewer rats, screeching.

And she became human,
a witness of ruined

becoming embodied,
reborn in water's womb.

Eclipse

Murder

They are calling,
all crows in night
like shattered walls of sound, flying
squawks, bursting in blackened sky.

Believe in it, the beckoning
of seeing the unmuted move,
to capture silence, belonging
to birds rising, waking the mist.

They killed it, disarranged water,
the drops of confusing fog
in a fleeting moment of thought,
lifted, afloat, away, silent.

Bird Strike

Wings up, beak underneath
    a shield for wind shear,
        crow shatters clarity
            into shards of wrong ways,
                turning driver to death.
Its head is crushed like ice,
    molten without shimmer
        over tires, blown out
            into a great bucket
                of nauseating punch.
And feathers fly over,
    turbulent, disordered
        in opaque glimmering,
            a gauze of fallen sky,
                blackening car finish.
Road crushes to convex,
    the wreck dredging the lanes,
        a highway of raptors,
            spearheaded and driven,
                a striking abstract.

White Out

To hunt pheasants in snow, father
awakens evergreens hiding
the fleeting of them, their feathers.

He shatters the sane with insane,
the blasting of branches of calm,
to smother the madness of them.

They burst like airbags in wreckage,
without a formal formation,
a disordered flight into death.

He aims at the airborne, before
the apex of one, opening
its body to him, to behead.

Blood splatters like a pureed sponge,
a bird fallen by force, pumping
red into white, by father's pulse.

Photo Shoot

Father is landing sky, assailing
pheasants in air, falling for beloved
memories developed in film, like clouds
burst open for him, shot fowl into scope,
piercing his eyes for photos of endings.

Prizes arranged for a picture of time,
a mosaic of bulleted bellies,
with wings overlapping, and legs arranged
like presidential forks, golden, polished;
they set everything in focus, an aim.

To capture it, shutter away the blood
in semiautomatic arrangement,
with powder frame and a steel hangar,
along with excess plumage for color,
he shoots a mountain of bones, embodied.

Sound Shot

Pathetic dreamer, look at its
bulleted wings, an acrobat
without a net of evergreens
to catch it, save it from splatter,
a bird abstract, in acrylic.

It cries like an organ off pitch,
classical moaning without time,
a bewail without a beat,
windless, and fading after fall,
punished for perpetual flight.

That air of a thing, the release,
a diaphragm dive, inhaled,
exhaled, and heaving
a great musical art, eagle
awake in the wind, mind blowing.

Walled, shot into a human,
where all wild die, inharmonic,
into this permanent nightmare,
grounded, muted on forest floor,
into a sound freedom, withdrawn.

Frostbite

Now this is frozen death, the dog,
a golden retriever in white
icicled with surrendered red;
the snow is making a mummy.

An enormous lump of absent
barking, no sound from the sunken,
as if winter had wasted it,
the puppy is muted in ice.

A crow is pecking the tail,
tempted by its disabled wag;
it will exhume an inhuman,
like a digger in a pet grave.

Pulling away at the hairy,
it unearths the ugly of it;
the ribs, the skull, the frosted teeth,
it all has been birded to death.

And soaring, the bird has bitten
and flown into the bloody frost
like an airplane through a body,
turbulent and tossed by its bite.

Glacial Sight

Cornea curves into iris, pupil
encircling into shivering lens,
like a whirlpool of anatomized sight,
specializing in animal ice
that traps creatures with optical cubes,
white cages of death in cold overflow,
to see winter with its icicle eye,
surveying death's frozen underworld,
to grasp what life's glacier envisions.

Colorblind Painting

There is an eternal
grayness in mountain glaze,
as if deliberate,
to draw you into white

before a careful black
scrapes sky with uneven
crags, sharp points to punish
air above for being

too blue, and beckoning
in this colorless life.
No green, not even grass
has primary pigments

within an absent gorge,
where bears are forgotten
and hunters are unseen,
delicate deletion.

Paint is perpetual
and reflecting water
below shadows of clouds
to sense color, its sight.

Ghost Writers

When angels arise in winter,
      snow reflects their sun shadow,
            outlines of the autograph gods.

Writing of everything ended:
      branches fallen on frozen ice,
            salmon caught in icicle streams,

birds broken by immobile wings,
      while ants bury in fallen hills,
            the blown silence of all nothing

rising into the ghosts, their wings
      tinted like cemetery stones:
            gray and white, with black lettering.

The scribes of seasonal scatter,
      detritus blessed by burials,
            in phantasmagorical light.

River Gift

Mother walks on water, a ghost
of moon giver, encircling.

Blue swallows white light, as drowning
appears in its making, a mold

of an interwoven woman,
as if sculpted by falling wind.

She folded in day, surviving
ashes of fire lightening

pitching into her forked body,
diving under watery drapes.

In this great palace of phantoms,
with ivory spotlights to sky,

we see her breathe over fathoms,
taken to a tower of air.

Late Spring

Ice crystals upon ancient boughs,
frozen nests beneath white blankets,
bark resembling witch fingers,
this is unwelcome winter, late
thaw in absent spring, with goshawks
shivering, in bitter silence.

The only loud is from losing
another oak in this frigid
timberland of forgotten sun,
a temple of forever moon
where worshippers are icicles,
bowing downward in snow penance.

Uproar, refuse bow, and be one
with cantankerous commotion,
break peace and summon summer,
the death of darkness in daylight,
in a sweaty pool of fervor,
springing hot, quelling cold, godlike.

Repellent

Castor oil within
our nevermore garden

of moles in marigolds,
souring temptation

with punitive layers
of laxative poison,

repulsive repellent
for the lick of a beast,

we besiege beloved
flowers with foul lacquer,

like coating a human
with inhuman rancor,

an awful blossoming
of impugnable pests

in putrid arrangement,
enraptured petals,

blooming adorable
orange and gold, the gifts

of our soiled god,
fertile, motherly.

Germinating Mice

Rodents in golden wheat,
they eat field, ending
our seeded life of earth,
as if ravenous germs.

They plunder proteins,
stealing spored growth,
essential nutrients,
bitten by mouse plague.

They digest the durum,
dreaming of fresh bread,
like children at dawn,
smelling semolina,

tempted by gilded air,
sensory pleasure;
mice pillage, so we snare,
grain, and mill, gutting gold.

Conquered

Anthill within hammers,
it nails to worn heads,
building a wall of earth
within overworked sand,
a mountain of labor
over constructed work.

Hours exhausted here,
hitting time after time,
to erect our castles
of wood, permanent homes
of glimmering varnish,
mansions of muscle.

Yet insects overwhelm
our colony of tools,
our laborious force
making a monument
of conquering man,
glory, the rise of it.

Abandonment

He opens the beaver, dissects
the impaled builder of dams.

He discovered it suffering,
sutured, and sinking in river.

It would not heal, with no hope
for life underwater, awash.

It smothers like a red abstract,
a painting of bloody pouring.

It pummels him, disarms his arms
like overpowering ocean.

He drops the dead, lets it languish,
abandoned beside shattered home.

A bear devours it, laps up
the nonliving, leaving the bones.

To welcome the hunter, it sniffs
the sink of him, his welling blood.

Gods of Thunder

On Rolling Thunder Day,
        a girl reads about gods
                while motorcycles roar.
Intake, carburetor,
        and fuel component parts,
                choppers sound like cloudbursts.
Unimaginable,
        they are shocking city,
                electrocuting roads.
They trample the tulips
        and pull out picketed
                fences, in firing.
Air cleaner coverings,
        along with filter kits,
                they siphon the sidewalks.
Like rioting devils,
        they are smashing windows,
                lighting curtains on fire.
While driving men to dust,
        women to willow to trees,
                they raze in wheeled storm.
Red rips through her window,
        setting story aflame,
                in angry utterance.
So she closes the book,
        learning how life ends,
                with roads rolling away.

The Getaway

Littered lawn, oil floating over,
like snakes over algae, reticulated
and netting green tentacles of grass
that carry spectacles of metallic rotors,
wheels, mufflers, filters, exhausting
air of engine steam, dire smoke,
moving a slithering man
through this disarrangement, making
an enemy of woman who walks over it,
criticizing his palace of silver, an away
from swallowing her sensual screaming,
her bite, at his everything wrong,
his breathing, boring, obese body,
as she caresses her beloved soil,
the land of her, wasted by his callused
accomplishment, his crust
on shimmering hands, his skin
shining molten opal, dissembled speed,
a safe of gear shifts, gathered and arranged
for dreamer, the god of sundown speed,
assembling him a getaway gift,
an escape to motorcycle moon.

Red Tide

At the Lighthouse

Moving out of spotlights,
life scatters in shadows.

Crustaceans under rotten kelp,
they hide, sand fleas overflown.

They wave with rolling waves
like a shoreline metronome.

Until shucking, creatures crack
open each other, shell shocked.

Battling bright, crabs
eviscerate to be unseen.

In emptiness, nothing
but organs bled over, beaming.

Ocean Effigy

That barrel is breathless,
smothered by carrying
oil, urchins, the heads
of decapitations,
the ends of everything.

Someone discovered it
swimming away to lose
to a leviathan,
smash in ocean squall,
erupt into pieces.

She summoned it, caught it
with a fishery hook
to employ its round form,
its laborious suave
carved into sturdiness.

Like the world offered all
to her, populations
of plentiful fishes,
she will wear out the wood
until its sides sever.

Tortured tool, overused,
it bursts like eaten bait;
she fires it, burns it
to ash, casts it away,
to welcome water death.

The Vessel

Salmon seep out of punch, the pulp
      of mussels and whale carcass,
            with seaweed slithering over.

She mixes a dead day, a taste
      of detritus and coral blooms,
            as if aging a gutted gin.

Everywhere, even eels,
      she mashes life into mayhem,
            flooding from her coveted vase.

She carries it, collects the sea
      and churns out the scales, the notes
            of seal howls and crab clamor.

They sink into her deep, her dark
      trove of torment, a rotten stew,
            reduced to a rainbow of death.

Delicious, she will boil it,
      digest it, eat life in acid,
            full of an ocean, fermented.

Without a Myth

It is a wrench in water squall,
our bow breaking in sea wake
of unbearable wind and rain;
we are tools for temperament.

In our sinking float, we bail
out the beast, its belligerent
batter and ram of us, waving
our world away, agitated.

It loves hate, inhuman hindrance,
as we sink into enormous
abyss, the mouth of its funnel;
and it is jiggling at us.

It grows into a great roar,
its reap of our vessel in half,
our heads downward, into heels,
taking life to live as a god.

Lost Undersea

An ocean diver, an engagement
of suspension over anemones,
pink and white fingers waving her away

to a gray mother lode of manatees
pointing to pestilent water, the wakes
of a shipwreck waiting for a woman

to enter and explore its sea swallow,
a rift of overgrown coral and crowds
of triggerfish, octopi, and sea clowns,

circling like acrobats, without air,
in an army of sea swells, the cycles
of a woman, disarranged, and lost

in sea luring, the love of it, a map
of misguidance, removed like a penguin
in snowstorm without an orderly way,

but the power of moving, the throttle
of currents awake in overboard rolls,
driving desire, speeding existence

in sailed ruins, a transformation
to being a believer in wreckage,
navigated to end in treasured squall.

Nightlights

Water lights wake like sea monsters
opening their eyes at midnight.

Blinking in the battering waves,
they spotlight trembling children.

The creatures sink into them, stuck
like blind spectacles, digested.

In phosphorescent entrails,
they beam within bodies, unbound.

Flooding in sanguine memories
of death, evoked in sleep, they bleed.

Awake, the young confuse ogres
by running every which way.

Smothering enlightened nightmares,
they escape into dark, dimming.

Glutton

Inside the orange
arms of the sea star,
a sandpiper siphons
the all of it, organs
and two stomachs.

It walks on eye spots,
searching for the spines
to break every back
and unnerve its system
with a spinal tap.

A wave reveals a universe
of suctioned legs,
exciting the giddy bird
like a gluttonous boy,
salted, sparkling, gifted.
.
So it smothers the pith,
an angry embalmer
of waved dead, relentless
with fowl tools, unfledged
to eat of endless growth.

The Drowning

She sinks it,
        making heavy
weight of light
        floating, the fall
of pufferfish,
        floored, deflated;
she fished for it,
        for undersea air,
a balloon to blow
        in sonic pop,
proving pain
        dives to death;
she sank it
        in wonderful
waking, the seep
        of organs exhaled,
releasing poison;
        she saved it,
sutured its skin
        and sucked
its self out,
        gifted gravity
by a girl
        with a point.

The Unraveling

Seal in straightjacket
    of cellophane seaweed,
like a magical trick,
    it strangles in webbing
of unfathomable
    fingers, caught, and moaning,
waiting for sea woman
    to unscramble awful,
a noose of castoff nets,
    a gagging magic rope
under a quarter moon;
    then she hears caterwaul,
mammalian music
    in nature's scorn, a night
turner in turbulent
    waving; she walks to it,
untangles the ugly
    binds of belligerent
ocean, offering
    a body to woman,
sculpted in water spell
    by this harbor on sand,
a salvation, set free.

Snail Bird

A snail kite is collecting
consumable creatures,

the meats of quagmire grass
within a shattering of shells,

as if a scavenger in swamp,
weeding throughout brackish water,

pecking away at innocent
newborns, the flesh of river flow.

It is an incessant, ceaseless
inhaling of dissections,

destroyed by bloody beak,
contented by the discontent

of spawn from an underwater
mother, gutted, eaten by bird.

It raises its mandible bill,
licks the lacquer, while ruffling

feathers over superfluous
openings, as if witnessing

nothing, unnoticed; it lofts,
avian, from aqueous birth.

Cannibals

Pipers dig life, engrained
under overwater,
siphoning sunken clams,
undertaking the tide.

A mother is making
an army of them, flocked
in shoreline camouflage,
hunting father, for food.

They gather geoducks,
shoring feet, by pecking
the pounds of them, like crabs
eating meat of the deep.

Bird blood in water sink,
a digestion of fowl,
they bite the lips of one,
a bivalve to bludgeon.

With salt, in fleshy waves,
they dig it up, drinking
its birded soup, chowder
sucked, boiling over.

So succulent, its skin
like a fathered disease,
they eat his assassin,
its appetizing chirp.

Starred Death

A boy is butchering sea stars,
chopping arms and dangling them.

He wears them for hair, magenta
interlaced with vermillion

squiggling into a façade
of sodium, a seasoning.

Where he eats at midnight, under
a blanket of night in the day,

he licks limbs, a murdered meal
of delight, chewing in darkness.

Inside, disobedience dies
and drifts to a new galaxy,

like a satellite lost in space,
where no one can discover him.

Until a mother ship moves in,
smelling a sensory ocean,

and disciplines his guts, the taste
of everything untamed, the awe.

Vogue

This is how to dissect seagulls:
split spinal cords through tracheas,
before ripping out the gizzards,
kidneys, lungs, and the bile ducts.

Remember to take home the beaks,
along with bushels of feathers;
you can braid them like extensions
of natural hair, organic.

Girls wear them like airborne witches,
playing with wings pointed to sky,
as if birds broke into fashion,
models in anatomized art.

Studying Loss

To wash away water, the drain
swallows its depth into earth sink,
a flush drinking lake into land.

Carp, yellow bass, and green sunfish
rise into sun, a dry burning
of fish, bleached within color bake.

Biologists observe the scene
like embalmers at a mud morgue
of intestines and swim bladders.

An ecosystem of caustic
sludge, systemically transplanted,
they plotted life's departure.

Gills, spleens, a cesspool of scales,
they flood into accurate counts
of trash, in scientific flow.

The Orbit

Here is my planet: a pocket
of air within water bubbles

fluttering in orbital flux,
the breakaway under a blue

rapid that churns itself to white
epiphany, a prolific

structure of turbulent flying,
like an airplane soaring in clouds

that burst over chaotic earth,
the constant nuisance of nature,

undone by speeding river,
shattered, tossed, tortured,

then silent, accelerated
and shocked in a forest of falls:

owls, deer, alders, and poison oak,
they died for wood deliverance,

witnessed by my falling orb,
an eye to watch inhumanity

while I disappear in my drop,
absorbed and running away.

The Breakthrough

All clear, and the ferry
has formed an inhuman
vessel, a water ghost
carrying silenced sound,
like a moonwalker's wave
moving so far away.

And the seals, unsung
in their absent rolling,
are asleep in the deep.
No seagull, not even
a slick eel around,
all life is nonliving.

A dead orca rises,
with blood canvassing skin,
red oil entrails.
It is spouting, open
to the undertaker,
that boat of butchering.

Dorsal to disfigured,
pectorals to trampled,
the ferry unfolded
exquisite embalmment,
captivating carnage
in tranquility's wake.

The Thinker

Inside the aquarium door there is a great white whale,
a ceramic centerfold in unlighted light,
with a glacier of penguins, seals, and seagulls
beside a sailor shop and sea center that sold
posters of every imaginable being, all institutionalized
like their biologist years ago. A ramp rises
to putrid tanks of amassed mold
that resemble cerebral lobes, where barracuda,
marlins, and morays swarmed among sharks
in corals that beamed fluorescent hues of electrified blue.

And then arctic ice appears in a polar world
of sablefish, salmon, and cod that twisted
like an underwater helix of scaled DNA,
carried away to research seasonal spawning.
A manatee pool arrives where awful cabbages
mound to feed an empty exhibit of white
vegetarian mammals, before the dark appears
in an unfathomable world of black. Nothing,
not even the sound of whooshing or smell
of rotten kelp is sensed in the room of nothing

alive, silent, as if thought escaped and left
only absent minded. Then round suctions appear,
orbs like moons in orbital space. Overlapping
in water muck, they pulse within neon silver
like planetoid rings, over and over, in a full tank,
forgotten and writhing alone. Lights flicker on,

revealing an enormous red octopus wrapped
around a triton like spaghetti around a fork.
Its gargantuan arms throb in acrid ink, agitating
bubbles with oblique clouds. One cephalopod eye

opens, focuses with iris, lens, and photoreceptor
cells that translate light into nerve signals
for its brain thinking about escape. And that scientist
handled it, grasped the octopod every minute,
hour, and day, staring into that eye, that eye,
watching, pulsing in cosmic hypnosis, through
the occipital entrance, down the street,
around the block, past a nurse reading
about bioluminescence, through the door, up the stairs,
to the cranial room of a subliminal man, immobilized.

Shadow

Peregrine

Unbound by binoculars
unable to witness
the departing dead,
you spark like gas flicker
setting grease to flame.

Faster, say field guides,
than cheetahs afire,
wind as your witness,
we cannot see you
dagger into duck.

Piercing through quack,
a beast into breasts,
you shoot mallards
like blasted guns,
sonic with fowl sounds.

God colored you gray,
with interwoven blue
to confuse carnage,
leaving untraceable
turbulence after death.

Rapid annihilation,
you bared bones for us
in bloody performance,
letting us languish
in sensory shadow.

Birdie

Grandfather executes
geese at the driving range
of death in the meadow,
a green painted with red

bodies, balled and gutted
like corpses without morgues,
open and atrophied,
off feathers, unfolded.

Show us the hole in one,
the hidden golf title
within your shot birdie,
a score for the beating

of players of fowl,
driven by bombardment,
in this great monument
of flights, grounded, and won.

Inheritance

Grandfather has a gift,
a forest canopy
shredded inside our barn,
our palace of woodchips,
hacksaws, and hay bales,
makings of a mover
who carried them over
to under, here to there,
in our forested hills,
as if a footprint god
gathered the world and walked
detritus through our door,
with sediment spilling
over our old bunker
of shoes and rotting rats,
our eagle and owl wings,
the carcasses of deer,
throbbing like a pressured
heart without blood thinners
on the edge of attack,
before rain waters breach
the waste of it, the guts
of gathered things, his kill,
steaming over spoils.

Appetizer

Caviar and crackers,
radishes in roses,
prosciutto piled
though shrimp cocktail crowns,
they spout like volcanic
eruptions of pleasure.

King salmon, pork bellies,
as well as wagyu steaks
and lamb lollipops
circulate like lassos,
tethering temptation
to prep our appetites.

For a great grizzly bear,
beheaded and bursting,
with a wide-open mouth
of jaws through rabbit ears,
it growls at the center,
this sight of its shooter.

Sound Bite

He collects salmon cakes, the sand
serving a platter to him, pink
and silver; they died suffering.

Wide open in wind, with his tongue
licking teeth cavities, his wet
mouth has captured seafood calling.

Like mice in a maelstrom, sound
beckons with squealing, fish eyes
squinting at him, he slices heads.

Carefully removing collars,
assigning bones to beach, he writes
a butcher's tale, eating ends.

Memory Fire

A chimney like a sky cannon
is shooting out of our ceiling,
a tower of clothing tatters,
burning in grandmother's furnace.

Underwear, overalls, sneakers
a needlepoint of partridges
and booties in primary blue,
they singe in a memory ball

of all of her gifts, the glitter
of plastic batons and trombones,
saxophones adorned with sequins,
a dazzling sight, set aflame

and rising into a cloud burst,
a boom into watery air,
smothered in the smoking of us,
a war of memories in flight.

Until the fall, the failing
of our unethical fire,
she disowns our inheritance
in a thunderstorm of ashes.

Going Out

Grandmother is pissing
in the fishing pool, the place
of a thousand trout
and no swimming signs.

In black and yellow,
her sunflower skirt
blossoms with speckled bees,
like a pointillist painting

thriving in a flied frenzy,
a pulse in summer sun,
with sweat beading down
her hatless head.

Grandfather grabbed it
at the brim, leaving
her boiling in water,
white to red in river

and without a rod
to cast in water waking
around her legs, with fish
pecking in the pooling

of urine and blistered toes,
like acid on iron,
her skin burning away
to release his catch.

He is gone, gifting
his secrets to her, to stand
in bottomless skirts, bright
in floral release, and going.

The Wine Wall

Beavers drink chardonnay
in a dam of winos,

a vintage of mammals
that roll into vineyards,

stealing the berries
of varietal sun.

Green, the seeded giver
of camouflaged skin,

as if they are building
a fermented fortress,

to wall an escarpment
of water, they hide it.

Throughout seasonal
change, they waken

ennui by intoxicating
timber, the brown of it,

with alcoholic mesh,
juicing ripened flow.

Mock Apple Pie

There is no grandmother
to core apples for us,

to split open sour
and douse it in sugar.

She took herself away
for some elderly crush

because he likes brownies
and prefers her dessert.

Crackers, sugar, and some
cinnamon, we found them

while looking for cookies,
as if they were unbaked.

All over, we mashed them
into a tart nightmare,

with sifted flour gowns
and baking powder shoes.

With gold smeared into white,
and then reformed in brown,

we baked a colossal
cake, instead of a pie.

She never ordered one,
ignoring us instead,

to flirt with her boyfriend
after grandfather died.

So we splatter spices,
ripening memories

of his liking, mocking
his recipe, the fruit.

Tapestry

The garden of worlds
      is growing
atmospheres
      of acquaintances:
hemlocks to pines,
      apples to plums,
and granite,
      the plantings of life
in a Mobius strip,
      blooming.
Tourists on
      a walking tour
with fanny packs
      and flipping flops,
children enchanted
      by smartphones,
and a drooling,
      unleashed poodle
are welcome
      within, eternal.
A smoking
      teenager, airborne
weed floating
      an evergreen high,
with a screaming
      infant craving
a cotton candy
      cloud, they peel

away mosses,
        as if welcome.
They are,
        even in off-seasons
with free admission,
        to be one
with nature,
        enrobed by patchwork
of sensual
        spaces, the pull
of it pushing
        them in, endless.

Kite

Technicolor tumor
steeped in cedar,
he sees
love in loft,
a boy breaking
branched
arms, retrieving
his father's craft,
killed.

With needles
puncturing palms,
he climbs
to its capture,
sparrows pecking
his jewel,
eating gifted
gold, life
gulped.

Incubator
with points,
it broods
feathered falls,
wings aloft,
blood
below, flowing
from family roots,
walled.

Wasted
like fresh pulp,
the seeker
surrenders,
sunken
by heirloom,
hindered
glow, gilt
high.

Prodigal

Going extinct, the art
     of dying for eaters
of their everything,
     bees comb into honey.
They slather in seeping
     gold, like millionaires
in a depleted mine,
     rolling in its riches.
She plunders it, the hive
     of endangered warnings,
like an heiress of death,
     enriched by pesticides.
Conquering colony,
     she grasps the heart of it,
opulent, pillaging
     original sugar.
Consumed in golden falls,
     pooling on stilettos,
she eats caloric sin,
     inherited wealth, spent.

Stinger

Today we grow poison:
oleander to ornament
our covering, our cave
of ancestral memories,
safe in sickening hive.

A haven on landfill,
it hides us, camouflages flesh
in green and pink, blossomed
in our neighborhood of nothing,
developed to brand new.

Bees pollinate our death,
our planted afterlife, solace
in house shatter, like ghosts
gathering stamens and haunting
houses with bitter stings.

Sour it, affix pain
to a punctured development,
targeting laborers,
the makers of torn dreams, sutured
by bloomed nightmares, deferred.

The Pest

Ivy is making a mummy,
a rat enrobed in green fever.

It smothers it, snaking in brown
and gray, suffocating its coat.

Like a body in gangrene gauze,
rodent rots within earthen weave.

It belongs to bound, citizen
of an immobilized city.

Watch it, arrowed, erupting
within cellular invasion,

an embalming of pestilence,
overgrown, virulent, creeping.

The Moss

Forest painted our house,
        flooded flooring,
smothered ceilings,
        in overpowering plague,
a fervent malady.
        No longer red, roof
mossed over, ripened
        to sickening green.
Blockaded, doors
        draped in disaster,
enclosing closets.
        Viewless, windows
shrouded, cloaked
        by virulent veil.
Silenced, bedrooms
        embodied overgrowth.
So we operated,
        became surgeons,
bestowed belongings,
        removed melanoma,
shucked covering,
        shined overshadow.
We cured, reclaimed
        cancerous skin,
healed.

Blinding

Silicone with a forever seal,
we chose the unbreakable caulk, keeping

elements away, protecting ourselves
while flown death rains from predatory sky.

Eagles, kestrels, and carnivorous hawks,
they loom over us, looking for loopholes

like spies in camouflage, waiting to bite;
so we smother the windows with midnight.

We squeeze outside of the lines, preventing
a peek on us, turning clear to opaque.

In sculpted still, we cloak ourselves with ooze,
to keep the raptors outside, concealed.

Hidden, we see blinded escape, afraid
of darkness, mobilized by black.

Milk

Cadaver in cream, we found it
in moon water where grandmother
washed overalls and underwear,
socks that succumbed to heels,
pants painted by hours of tar,
the tattered clothing of grandfather
filling the well of a woman
who dreamt of a world without night,
where sun rose over earth shadow
and framed a family of gold,
gone, when a husband surrendered
to heart attack death, the dying
of a lover in arms that washed
away in this coalesced pool,
layered in limestone and rain,
mixed into mired immersion
of a body in ground, a god
of coal and shale eruption,
appearing under drowning lace,
wrapping wife in mummified white.

Kindling

Lights without electricity
flare in odd ways, like collisions

of interstellar explosions,
unable to control flaring.

Red runs in every which way,
searing cedars like ironed skin.

We point at pulsations, each shock
perplexing us with displacement,

absorbed in alternating night;
we fall into the elements.

Fuel, oxygen, and energy
enrapture us, igniting all

into an orb of brilliant
burning, ceased, insurmountable.

Twisters

Here is the end of us,
  a museum of dust,
    wanting to wash away.
Tornadoes threw houses,
  boulders into bathrooms,
    like a fierce sky riot.
Blended, our kitchen shook,
  disposed of, in a hole
    of tiles and turkey.
Our garden grew tulips,
  clipped into yellow rows
    that flew upward in wind.
At least return water,
  wash out our collection,
    in catastrophic sink.

Rebirth

See the cemetery
exposing lineage,
revealing lifelines.

Its buried melt winter,
sinking snow within sun,
granting life to the dead.

Obelisk, upright, slant,
graves mark lost families
born into morning growth.

Granite, concrete, and lime,
they wake with unrest,
the surging of summer.

Whispering in the wind,
phantoms in shadow song
burn the frozen away.

Turn life, transition us
and steal soullessness,
make ghosts unforgotten.

The Takeaway

That said, we all become water,
bodies diving into great blue
horizon, a solitude home
        in waterfall, enlightened
        in floating arms of freedom's wake,
        perpetual motion, moving
                our sails away, our escape
                from an earth after erasure,
                navigating by homing moon.

Acknowledgements

"Moon Highway" *Ginisko Literary Journal*
"Solidarity" *Nassau Review*
"White Out" *Cold Mountain Review*
"Sound Shot" *The Wayfarer*
"The Vessel" *Carolina Quarterly*
"Snail Bird" *Free State Review*
"Inheritance" *Midwest Quarterly*
"Memory Fire" *Midwest Quarterly*
"Going Out" *Saranac Review*
"Kite" *Permafrost*
"The Pest" *Carolina Quarterly*
"Milk" *Kestrel*

Thank you to Ed Byrne, Juan Morales, Amy Nawrocki, and Barrett Warner for their enduring support. Thank you to my colleagues at the Bread Loaf Environmental Writers' Conference and Johns Hopkins for their valuable expertise. Thank you to the literary magazines that published selections from this collection. And thank you to my family for their everlasting encouragement.

About the Author

Andrew Jarvis is the author of *Sound Points, Ascent, The Strait,* and *Landslide.* His poems have appeared in *Cottonwood, Evansville Review, Valparaiso Poetry Review, Tulane Review,* and many other magazines. He was a Finalist for the 2014 Homebound Publications Poetry Prize, and he has received several honors from the INDIE Book of the Year Awards. He also received Silver Medals in Poetry from the Nautilus Book Awards and CIPA EVVY Book Awards. Andrew holds an M.A. in Writing from Johns Hopkins University.

HOMEBOUND PUBLICATIONS

Ensuring that the mainstream isn't the only stream.

At Homebound Publications, we publish books written by independent voices for independent minds. Our books focus on a return to simplicity and balance, connection to the earth and each other, and the search for meaning and authenticity. Founded in 2011, Homebound Publications is one of the rising independent publishers in the country. Collectively through our imprints, we publish between fifteen to twenty offerings each year. Our authors have received dozens of awards, including: *Foreword Reviews'* Book of the Year, Nautilus Book Award, Benjamin Franklin Book Awards, and Saltire Literary Awards. Highly-respected among bookstores, readers and authors alike, Homebound Publications has a proven devotion to quality, originality and integrity.

We are a small press with big ideas. As an independent publisher we strive to ensure that the mainstream is not the only stream. It is our intention at Homebound Publications to preserve contemplative storytelling. We publish full-length introspective works of creative non-fiction as well as essay collections, travel writing, poetry, and novels. In all our titles, our intention is to introduce new perspectives that will directly aid humankind in the trials we face at present as a global village.

WWW.HOMEBOUNDPUBLICATIONS.COM

CPSIA information can be obtained
at www.ICGtesting.com
Printed in the USA
FFOW03n1900070518
46536027-48506FF